For an Aquari-
poetry love
could be
th
" The Sign of The [barcode: CW00495163]

There's no particular poem
to describe how I feel but
lots of lines describe me
in part.

Love

Al
xxx
xx
x

Heather Buck

The Sign of
The Water Bearer

Anvil Press Poetry

Published in 1987
by Anvil Press Poetry Ltd
69 King George Street London SE10 8PX
and 27 South Main Street Wolfeboro NH 03894 USA

This book is published
with financial assistance from
The Arts Council of Great Britain

Set in Joanna
by Bryan Williamson, Manchester
Printed in Great Britain
at The Arc & Throstle Press, Todmorden, Lancs

British Library Cataloguing in Publication Data

Buck, Heather
   The sign of the water bearer.
   I. Title
   821'.914   PR6052.U24/

Library of Congress Cataloging-in-Publication Data

Buck, Heather.
   The sign of the water bearer.

   I. Title.
PR6052.U249S5   1987   821'.914   87-1036

ISBN 0-85646-193-8 (pbk.)

FOR HADLEY

ACKNOWLEDGEMENTS

Acknowledgements are due to the editors of the following periodicals where some of these poems appeared for the first time: *Acumen*, *Agenda*, *Critical Quarterly*, *Encounter*, *English*, *The Julian Meeting Magazine*, *Other Poetry*, *Outposts*, *The Rialto* and *Sorbonost/Eastern Churches Review*.

Contents

'I do not imagine that in my reflections on the meaning of man and his myth I have uttered a final truth, but I think that this is what can be said at the end of our æon of the Fishes, and perhaps must be said in view of the coming æon of Aquarius (the Water Bearer), who has a human figure and is next to the sign of the Fishes. – The Water Bearer seems to represent the self. With a sovereign gesture he pours the contents of his jug into the mouth of *Piscis austrinus*, which symbolizes a son, a still unconscious content.'

C.G. JUNG, Memories, Dreams, Reflections

The Church of Agia Theodora, Arta

Inside there was enough quiet
to accommodate the sound of candles
spluttering near her shrine,
of metal quivering against metal
in the line of hanging lamps,
and words that flesh themselves
when the mind untethered
from its own unending chatter
dares to leave itself alone.

Meeting at Monemvassia

Inside your house a leafy court
where songbirds plucked their final frenzy
from withdrawing light, a darkened hall,
and silence like a great invasion from the sea,
peace that infiltrated, took you utterly.

You were wearing it that afternoon of heat
when cats stirred only for necessity,
as in the stillness it enfolded me.

Sitting on the wall you told me how a snake
lay coiled beside the church, how snakes
have always guarded treasure.
But in that atmosphere it seemed
that fighting dragons was some queer disease
born out of restlessness, born out of need
for anything that's absent, that is not now.

Was what we shared the treasure? That lack
of striving, that entire abandonment
to everything that is. So singular,
that even as I write I'm losing it
by wanting Monemvassia.

Lintel in the Museum at Nikopolis

'Dorotheus and Marcella have erected it
to fulfil their promise' – 1st-2nd c. AD

Did they wreathe it with vines
and see the flagstones beneath
take on a patina of polish
from their own, and smaller
quick running feet, forcing
even the stones to acknowledge
their passage backwards and forwards,
in and out of the trauma of living?

And did they learn by sharing
each other, not to tip too much
of the discourse of self
in the spaces between, but leave
enough light and air to grow
like trees to shelter each other?

Meteora – Monasteries of the Air

As the shades of evening assembled,
the monasteries began to float as if
they had sailed to the surface of some
private element.
> PATRICK LEIGH FERMOR, Roumeli

Monasteries perched
on pinnacles of quiet,
where plunging cliffs slide
immeasurable depths,
enough for the eagle's
shadow to sail,
for the snail's smear
of a spring's overflow
to ribbon its way
to the valley below.

Where raised voices
jostling the immediate air
dissolve on thick
blotters of mist,
or melt into clouds
like mushrooms wreathing
giant stalks of stone.

At night solitary
unmoving lights,
seemingly balanced on air,
signal the bearded monks
are at prayer,
threading their minds
into spheres where
sight, speech and thought
are broken rungs
on a ladder of love.

Pilgrimage to Dodona

Necessary perhaps for the pilgrimage
to pack all my fears and anxieties,
stuffing their awkward shapes into deep
recesses of luggage, hoping they
wouldn't bulge into the public places.

Only letting them out in hotels where
the noise of the plumbing hadn't that easy
fit to a mind tuned to the nightly
shifting of an old house settled to sleep.

Pressing their jagged spikes to my sides
on the high mountain climb, where the smell
of goat reached into the back of the car,
and tinkling sheep browsed beside shepherds
well-tutored in violence of lightning and storm.

To the steep-sided valley where ancient
bare-footed priests used to reap
words from whispering oak-leaves, binding
and braiding them into fragile responses
solid enough for pilgrims petitioning gods.

Was it the staring implacable sun
or the collapse of man's faith into reason
that scoured away powers and presences,
and left the whine of a thin empty wind
listlessly shaking a few sterile leaves?

And was it the blunt eye of faith in need
of resharpening that prompted the journey?

Icon

Icon from which there emanates
a kind of radiance
in which the best of all the mind's
intentions are contained,
a promise of a full and total
giving at the end.

She leans, a laden basket in her arms
to brush her lips against her Lord's
rough painted crucifix,
and for one moment to allow her mind
relief from its erosions,
a dumb apology
for all the necessary claims
that edge him from her love.

Uncertain whether pain and loss
would at last ensure
he has the space
to flower in her heart.

Apple Harvest on Mount Pelion

Apples so big that no mouth
could shape itself to their size,
so plentiful that peasants put off
eating and sleeping, turning
their lives inside out till the last
of the giant all-night lorries
had rumbled away through narrow
cliff-hanging lanes that scrambled
down the side of the mountain.

Not only thundering lorries
skimmed off the last layers of sleep,
but moonlight, scouring the bedroom
of darkness, summoned us to a view
of a world dropping away,
of men growing smaller, remote
in streets hung with cobwebs of light.

Provençal House 1966-80

The Writing on the Wall

A turn in the road and there it stood,
backing away from human knowledge,
as if its cultivated negligence
could deceive the foreign eyes that pried;
German invader, chance tourist, equally
it shunned their sabotage.

How dared we tangle lives with that
most reticent of dwellings, barely house,
that sheltered casual labourers, a horse,
who knows what else, all that was in the past.
Now darkness owned it, closed shutters
concealed the mouse, spiders busy
at their webs, and scorpions that trod
the darker cracks of that abandonment.

There was a strange insistence, a sudden
need to be a part of that great solitude;
to know the flaring sun, the ample stars,
the mistral's unvarying persistence,
to know the shadow on a ruined wall,
a place so overgrown it seemed that
rose accommodated grape,
and hips were lavished on the vine.

Then as we pushed the door against
uncounted years' neglect, light picked its way
across the earthen floor, slid up the wall
revealed an empty manger and a black
crayoned scrawl, 'Jacques Touvel mort à Verdun'.
Sobered we paused, for half a century,
another war had come and gone,
and clouds were gathering again
in those uneasy pools, the minds of men.

First Summer, 1968

In twenty months it was the scorpion
no longer dared, or thistle force
the kitchen floor; and spider's webs were
flimsy veils soon set aside. Brisk winds
absconded with the smell of rotting straw,
dispatched the staleness in the hall.

But reticence was slow to yield, as though
the house was hoarding silence, and every
barking dog, each footless wind, the voices
in the field were momentary digressions
that returned each time to silence.

It is a trick of man's imagination
to think his own time singular, but
tanned by centuries of sun, the Roman
monuments remained to question such
pretensions. And in the sculptured stone
of Arles and St. Remy, Marius and his men,
till then old rumours from an ink-stained text,
at once assumed reality.

But we were apron-stringed to now
when Russian tanks were rolling into Prague.
Coffee and croissants in the sun
and bitterness upon the tongue.

September 1973

There were no easy exits from ourselves.
We learnt to live with mountains at the door,
not distanced to the bottom of the street
by the need to hear the gossip
of anxious women with their shopping.

These were days to sit by, days we measured
by the need to hug the plane tree's shade
while the hot pursuer climbed towards its peak.
Days to give uneasy stirrings time to brink,
as when a pool quietens,
reveals those things one would forget.

And when a bird's wing shadowed on the ground
had gone before our eyes could reach its substance,
or when a lizard robbed our expectations
by its flight, they were a part of living,
a part of all desire, all pain, all loss.

Sound of gunfire in the field at dawn,
as though the grief refused to sleep, and must
assert itself in nightmare. Those tales
Resistance heroes told of how the savage
Butcher jerked his puppet-strings from Lyons
are history now. It was *la chasse*,
and rows of thrushes drying in the sun
hang there instead of men.

Interlude

The year the clanking bucket drank the well
quite dry, when sunflower ghosts were loitering
in the lane, and oleanders shrank
to drained and listless shadows of themselves,
it seemed the house received us to itself.

The terrace pulsed with insects and with heat
and only lizards skimmed its stones. And when
we went inside and saw light filtering
the stiffened gauze at windows, and throw
its wavering branches over walls
and whitened ceiling, it was like water
moving on the vaults of old stone bridges.

The Building of the Missile Base

The year the lorries came, as though they climbed
the darkest inclines of a prophecy,
they stirred the dread we didn't dare confess.

But were we acquiescent then? Remarking
how a lane was widened here, a village bar
enjoyed increased prosperity, and
as a cat disturbed in sleep will stretch
and turn and sleep again, we drowsed
a few more summers in the sun.

But sound of protest growing steadily
cut through our lethargy, we saw
how fragile was our tenancy of peace.

So how to live, the dread confessed, as though
the doors would always open on the street,
as though the bride who danced
this August afternoon would one day sit
an aging gossip in the sun?

The Egg Seller

A nun or peasant selling eggs?
I ask her in to ease the tiredness
in her eyes, and wonder if the dawn
was threaded with her prayers,
or if when first light traced
the edge of candle-stick and bed
she nudged the husband at her side,
and hurriedly attired herself
to warm his coffee and his bread.

Fine wool in folds about her face,
a simple coif without the lace,
hands at rest in one another
as though they long ago had learnt to stay
themselves in readiness. Either way, whether
her path to cottage or to convent lay
they would untwine themselves for love.

Spring

This tattered beggary,
this bird-chewed crocus
that carries hope
beyond the scope
of its small statement,

so insignificant
that one might miss
its place upon the path
of winter turning into spring,

except that light is carving
out a portion from the night
to make a wider
definition of the day.

Ownership

Fully involved with every brush stroke,
each new artist's work, he bought his paintings
with discernment, taste. And when he hung them,
each one's setting, each surrounding space
was chosen to advance its own perfections.

But one he never hung, a window facing south,
where mountains crowded far horizons,
and clouds with life-styles of their own
would take to wandering off as soon
as he had grouped them. Where blackbirds mocked
him with their flight, and every morning's
offering of blue gave way to sudden squalls.
Where mists came winding down from mountains,
steamrolling through the sun and leaving him
disconsolate and dark.

He'd sometimes seen a picture where paint
had trespassed from the canvas and spilled
along the frame, not wastefully, but as though
the artist's vision could not be amputated
by a frame. But here, his window frame,
as stern as any guillotine, permitted
no such overflow of life.
His goldfish bowl had left him dispossessed.

Concentration of Hands

(Barbara Hepworth)

A morning in the Tate, sheltering from rain
to weave again the same
elaborate pavane among the ones
who visit each and every work of art
and those who stay a moment and depart.

And so I've come to this, to stand and stare,
to leave, and then return once more
to this one drawing
which grafts me to the same piece of floor.

A concentration of skilled hands, some four
or five that tie and tether him to life.
So still his form, suspended in a shaft
of time that afterwards his mind
will never visit. Instead he'll wake
as from a sleep to gather up the pain
and orchestrate his life again.

The Convalescent

(by *Gwen John*)

Convalescent you may be,
and fragile looks your tenancy
of that frail shell,
but within a self
as finely turned as any filament
essential to a glass lamp's
incandescence.

Madonna

(by Dame Elizabeth Frink, in Salisbury Close)

She will not wait for me.
No longer bound in alcoves
of the mind or in the naves
of tall cathedrals, she strides,
independent as the air,
her flying skirts dispersing
dust-layered images.

All time has made her wait,
a glitter of candles at her feet,
hearing the heavy door
stun noises from the street,
her stage-paste effigy
provoking dumb confusions
and prayers that falter
on a rack of doubt.

Now she leads along untrodden tracks.
Huge suffering has mapped her face
and gullies of pain
have seamed that country.
Compassion is no stranger there
but even so a knot
of tributaries about the eyes
is fed by laughter. A thousand
shadows at her back: in front
purpose breaks from her like light.

The Curé d'Ars

Those flagellations, fasts and body torments
are out of fashion now, their quaint excesses
carry scentings of martyr's blood congealing
on arena floors, a crowd's great roar.

They were the root to which you clung,
their long and wiry tentacles
descending to the darkness where love sprang.

How else could all those broken minds
and limbs be healed, except by scalping out
a space within yourself to nourish them.

A twisted thing upon a crutch was what
you always saw, the withered fruit of hours
spent at doors of healing shrines, like those
who missed the Prophet's path in Palestine,
were left to wring sweet-sour days from pain.

But some retrieved from you their limbs
to know again the feel of mud that spattered
up from puddles, to rip untidy sounds
from dry, discarded leaves, and left their crutches
clawing like bats upon your walls,
quiet braggers of your secret ecstasies.

Petrarch at Fontaine de Vaucluse

Was it here my love began to fatten
in its solitude, and ripen into words?
Here, in this small garden where the large
and brooding laurel stands; a sapling then,
inadequate to shield me from the scorching
mid-day sun, as Laura's frugal favours
were too thin for nourishment.

A dream that fleshed itself in solitude,
too easily dissolved by heavy feet
that plodded to my door with baskets
full of aubergine and wine. Ill-timed
reminders that absence does not print the ground,
as were the little excavations in the earth
from cats promiscuous among my vines.

I made the waters of the Sorgue
a flowing screen on which to sketch desire,
an insubstantial mirror where she walked
with me, as vulnerable to clouding
as the mind to doubt. And yet if days
went by without event on which to trace
a pattern of myself, I hurried
to the court at Avignon to find
that clearer outline vanity requires.

But always I returned; mine was a love
that made an instrument of absence
and learnt to play its complex songs
upon unsatisfied desire.

Emily Dickinson

How many years you lived in silent rooms,
three pairs of hands might yield as many fingers
as you'd need to total them. And yet
how strong to purge your life of human
intercourse because you feared
it might disseminate your essence.

You let your mind become so uninhabited
that vagrants used it, lodged nights among
your fears, left unlocked doors
the wind abused, and you plucking
nervously at certain kinds of dawn
that had no kinship
with the disposition of the clouds.

And though the garden shouldering its loads
of snow compounded your bleak solitude,
as nuns wrap walls around themselves
to dull the chattering world,
you cultivated silence to hear the words
that always stalked you, no matter how
their impetus for flesh bruised you.

The Shattering

There is this hard shoulder
jutting into my life,
and the intolerable sea-thrust
that wears it away.

It seems that time doesn't vary
the incident, only darkens
and toughens the texture.
We are so vulnerable
we stand back
from the shattering.

But consent to stay
within its fragments, know
that at the hub of darkness
is this hollowed place
to cradle light.

The Cage

Like a shawl thrown over a cage
of singing birds is the dark falling
on trees full of birdsong at dusk.

As the sudden awareness of age
when the stunned ear refuses
all laughter and sound.

Singing birds signal the light
with a tumult of song, is there
no quick lifting of shawls
from the cage?

The Unheeded Self

That unmuddled self of sleep is one
my mind on waking cannot reach, unless
a blowing strand of dream is caught upon
a hook of thought. Then to put my hands
on warm reality, that strange yet so
familiar coat that I find hanging there.

Shadow Figures

for *Carl Gustav Jung*

Two men before they turn to face the day
fold up their beds like shadows rolled away,
and brush the intervening air of stale
hostilities that dreams have stranded there.

There is a muddy centre where the shadows prowl,
patrol the undergrowth at night, and then
at daybreak crouch there scenting prey
ready to pounce on innocent intruders,
the ill-timed words that will not go away.

But stay where childhood fits of grief still rage,
as storm-clouds overcast a summer's day,
and where the mind continually
deforms the present with remembered pain.

Where flashing shields still turn the sunlight back,
repulsing light, like double-sided mirrors
each relaying repetitions of the self,
the old confusions never sorted out.
Where is the enemy? Outside the palisade,

or within? This clouded outline
on the glass, this smudge of dust
that tarnishes the shield's much battered bronze,
this enemy within who twists and turns
a spectral knife in phantom wounds.

Old man, you set us to explore
the geography of self, bequeathed us charts
to lead us through those dark interiors,
and showed us at the end a place of light,
the golden roses growing in our porch.

Self Knowledge

Of all most difficult the years
when we unwind the colours of the self,
unwind, and wind them up again
until some unity, some matching

of the inner with the whole
resolves the clash of differing moods,
when spreading stains no longer blemish
other lives that touch the rim.

For like chameleons we learn
to match and tone with everything
around, without betrayal
of the self which cost so dear.

The Lorries

On Christmas Eve he scoured the silences.
Not for the muddle of footsteps stamping
in the snow, nor for the doors
that shut on voices; not even
for the fabled sleigh-bells, or sudden
hammering of church-bells on dumb air.

What roused him was the sound of lorries
cresting unknown hills, threading rutty lanes
until, his hopes receding, distance
severed them from him.

All his life the lorries came. Sometimes
he heard one coming up the hill, and saw
it hesitate beyond the garden wall.
Some hasty commerce in the hall,
a parcel left, and then a pause,
it would accelerate and leave,
bereaving him of what its presence promised.

His childhood past, they would arrive
to transport all the baggage of his life
to other sites, the mounting register
of things achieved he needed
to impress himself and others. The drawers
he'd stuffed with furtive happiness,
the desks on which ambition wept,
and beds in which too many nights had forced
unwilling knowledge of their emptiness.

Always when the lorries left they took
their secret, until the last of all
his moves when waiting as an actor
in the wings, it seemed there never
was a moment when the curtain rose
or magic prop that would transform a scene.

Loss

Hearing last night the perfect song,
the voice trembling on the final C,
I knew loss is conceived in the ecstasy,
and the one certainty
the wind snatching voraciously.

Till only the lightest evocation
remains, as gestures left over
from loves that have ended.

Separate

Wandering over uneven streets
treading stars into pools after rain,
it's the same world we are walking
and yet when we meet
each is reporting a difference,
only events are tied,
everything else moves away.

Now

This is the bankrupt hour,
when the mind begins to weigh
the crowded past against an unused future,
and disallows the possibility of now.

When drawn and puckered curtains
seem a fencing in, and silencè
not a positive denial of noise,
but a quicksand for the mind to wander in.

It is the cat who leaves no joy unspent,
uncurls herself from sleep
to rub her tongue along her fur,
then overturns with waving paws
to pluck a moment from the air.

Evening

Flushed dark as aubergine, the evening waits,
a hesitation in the day
when files and copy-books are packed away,
and girls in offices shake off
the tyranny of telephones,
for they inherit hours like rooms
which they inhabit and call their own.

The time when traffic swells and car doors slam,
as when a chapter springs to life,
the story moves, the idling mind
forgets the scuttle needing coal,
relaxes into bliss again.

When in an opened bottle wine
begins to seek its own decline,
and in a quickening of words
two lovers shed their separateness
and in each other lose themselves.

When through the railings of the park
the trees dissolve in smears of darkness,
and quizzing fingers of the wind,
like hands that ransack jumble,
frisk the pillowed leaves for tramps.

The Door

Light

Where sunsets were hearsay
and swifts unremarked,
where planners had parcelled
the great fields of wheat
into plots for our lives,
where iron birds full of faces
were climbing to skies
eroded by buildings,

a trap-door opened
one autumn night
throwing down
long ladders of light
for the mind to soar
through a leap of stars
to a blazing carnival
night of fire.

If a circus had moved
the following day
it would have left
an acre of trampled
and upturned turf
where the big-top had shaken
its roots from the earth,
and the sound of the clapping,
the cheers,
would have echoed and died
in a thousand ears.

But the only sounds
were of starlings gossiping
under the eaves,

the wind mauling
October leaves.
The cold day had carried
the vision away,
had plundered
the lights and the magic.

Withdrawal

Imprisoned by schedules of trains,
by annual replacement of bulbs,
by houses all different
but looking alike,
and by the indifferent heels
that drummed isolation into the bone,
so that the garden fence
and the garden gate
hindered none
for no one approached.

Wrapped in a tissue of abstinence
for nothing attracted,
nothing appealed,
only the desert approached
and the white sand crept
under the floor-boards
into the skirting
behind the eyes
and into the brain,
until at mid-day sometimes
the vision,
compelling, remote,
burned like a mirage
in the throat
of a terrible fire.

And so it went on,
life ill-nourished
by meetings on pavements,
vague conversations,
distractions, evasions,
a dreadful ennui settled
into the tea-cups
while the mind fidgeted
wandered away.

Lying awake,
pushing around in the brain
odd scraps from books,
from those travelling
the same uncomfortable pain,
a mind's archaeology
which the fingers
ached to explore,
but the tools rusted,
the door remained.

Fed by the Ravens

They were not punctual or spry
my ravens,
dropping out of a morning sky
spilling bread and fresh meat
from their beaks,
and although I tired my eyes
for signs of their coming,
I always found them
too near the cliff-edge
feeding me knowledge
of other men's hells.

So that footprints on paths
dark, unfrequented,
and clusters of candle-flames
burnt on to beams of houses
empty, untenanted,
showed that someone had breathed,
had walked in the spaces,
was turning the corner
a pace or two on.

Learning a Language

Nights were bizarre
and inscrutable
filled with the vagabond
language of dreams,
until I discovered
the symbols and signs
scribbled on gateposts
were motifs
old as the myths of mankind.

The Return

Never again were ladders let down.
Slowly light splintered in
through small cracks in the door
trailing the strangest of blossoms,
and yet –
they were the same
violets and roses I'd always known
except that a different light
distinguished them.

As though through the years
I'd looked the wrong way
and missed
the way light handled
the silken quilt,
or frescoed a trellis
of leaves on the ceiling,
and the way pain and sorrow
would suddenly twist
into unaccountable bliss.

Now pages of print
dull and dry to the eye
flamed and leapt into life,
and the path that had dithered
into the place where
ghosts of the mind
wander backwards and forwards
in and out of the labyrinth
had cleared once again.

A great many faces
crowded the house,
talking their way into spaces
the ghosts had vacated,

and glasses empty and shelved
were suddenly flushed with red wine.
But under the talk and the laughter
the candles burn steadily on.

Distractions

Summer devours us with distractions,
as near as the shrub-rose at the door,
the hubbub in the hall.

But when the wounded sun lies in the earth,
and fold after fold of snow is unskeined
from the sky, there is time
to contemplate the winter
in the absence of the human voice,
in the silence of the empty hall.

Strange to find silence itself so noisy with sound.
Does the ear seek
the wind's complaint under the door,
the little draught playing in the chandelier?
Is it fear that twitches and writhes
in the shadows, furnishes
the dark corner with threats?

And afterwards the inner debate.
Silence made loud with interminable discourse.
Nowhere to escape the trivial self chattering,
no landscape inviolate from the tip
of one's own smouldering rubbish.

Perhaps only the privileged find it.
The mystic's void scraped to a flawless
perfection, or the tortured few
in their suffering's grossest extremity
find they're no longer alone.

The Inaccessible Jewel

For myself, the inaccessible jewel
is the normal and all of life, in
poetry, is the difficult pursuit
of just that.
             WALLACE STEVENS

Always so high so out of reach,
as when a sunset tips
the tallest fountain with its fire,
absurd this metaphor of where
the human mind sets radiance.

Or where the rarest ivory lies
behind locked doors, and where
the keeper of the key
reluctantly, at certain hours
draws back the door and notes
the disappointment in our eyes.

Are we all tourists searching for
the singular, particular,
instead of looking where
the fussy tractor sweats with oil,
its wake of gulls
billowing out white feathery foam,
or where the lines of furrows break
for pools to house
the mirrored fragments of a sky.

Things As They Are

Simply to live, to live for what?
For the marigold that flames within the pot,
for squares of sunlight patching shabby cars,
for things exactly as they are.

Why must I wrest a meaning from the stars,
confuse the loveliness of plant and sky
by setting what I think and feel
between their bare existence and my eye?

Immediate and present are the pebble
and the clay to the child at play,
while I, as if I took a soup-spoon
to the world, must test and weigh
the taste of everything before I drink.

To an Old Professor

i.m. P. Gurrey

O degli altri poeti onore e lume,
vagliami il lungo studio e il grande amore,
che m' ha fatto cercar lo tuo volume.
                    DANTE, Inferno 1, 82-84

The shadow of your aging head
has loitered often near these words,
neat pencilled notes still track the places
where your mind once squirrelled for its ecstasies.

A taste for excellence was what you sowed,
as often in the garden with the weight
of years upon you, eyes half-closed
and Dante slipping to your knee,

you'd wake and read aloud to me,
and words would come among my thoughts
as though my understanding danced at last
to their unrivalled leading.

At times the bronze chrysanthemums
would loll and stagger in the autumn heat
until your trembling hands
formed splints to bear their ragged heads.

And when we listened to a song-thrush in your trees
it tore great frenzies from a throat
accustomed to more reticence,
or when you picked a rose, it was of all
most singular, supremely gold. A gift
to make small humble things unique,
to colour and immortalize my world.

Prisoners

for Hadley

I think of prisoners sitting
in dark empty cells
and footsteps that swell
their abysses of terror,
and know that sanity is rigged
upon the underpinning
of habitual things.

In light that furnishes
the outlines of familiar rooms,
the steady rhythm of the cat's
responsive purr,
the unstinting generosity
of the thrush that sings.

In the touch of fingers
gliding over polished wood,
and in the happiness
of your hand reaching out
for mine I know the depths
of my dependence,
and welcome
the captivity it brings.